PRAISE FOR *SHE STOOD FOR FREEDOM*

"*She Stood for Freedom* tells the story of Joan Trumpauer Mulholland, an ardent, devoted fighter for the cause of equal justice. The desire she had to right the wrongs of her country took her from a college campus to downtown street demonstrations and then to jail. She truly deserves the descriptor 'foot soldier' having lived the life of one while standing for freedom in the only way she knew she could. The book is a testament to both Joan and the many other unknown individuals who worked so hard to accomplish so much."

—Birmingham Civil Rights Institute

"This readable, fast-paced narrative illustrates why a young white woman would feel compelled to join the Civil Rights Movement of the 1960s. It was simple, actually: she was a Southerner, a Christian, an American and it was the right thing to do."

—William Pretzer, Curator, Smithsonian National Museum of African American History and Culture

"Martin Luther King Jr. once said, 'One day, the South will recognize its heroes.' Joan Trumpauer Mulholland is one of those heroes. You cannot tell the story of America's Civil Rights Movement without talking about the sit-ins, the Freedom Rides, the March on Washington, the 16th Street Baptist Church bombing, Freedom Summer, and the Selma to Montgomery march. How amazing in this book to tell all those stories through the life of one woman—Joan Trumpauer Mulholland, whose uncommon courage and unflinching perseverance continue to inspire us all."

—Jerry Mitchell, winner of more than 20 national journalism awards for his reporting on the Civil Rights Movement

"A wonderfully written book about a wonderful, worthy hero. An individual who I greatly admire."

> —HANK THOMAS, Civil Rights activist, one of the original Freedom Riders, one of the founders of the Student Nonviolent Coordinating Committee

"*She Stood for Freedom* will help young people understand that 'ordinary' people like Joan Trumpauer Mulholland were as important to the successes gained during the Civil Rights Movement as better known players like Rosa Parks and Dr. Martin Luther King Jr. Her story also illustrates that you are never too young to do the right thing. This book will help young people better understand how they too can be heroes and stand up for justice and equality for all people."

> —TERRI LEE FREEMAN, President, National Civil Rights Museum

"It was my privilege to meet Joan Trumpauer Mulholland in 1961 when she helped the nonviolent, civil rights activists prepare for their risky, interracial bus ride from Washington, DC, to the heart of the deep South. ... This well-written and beautifully illustrated book is one to be savored and shared with future generations who may need to look within themselves for similar courage."

> —SIMEON BOOKER, award-winning journalist and author of *Shocking the Conscience: A Reporter's Account of the Civil Rights Movement*

SHE STOOD FOR FREEDOM

SHE STOOD FOR
FREEDOM

THE UNTOLD STORY OF A CIVIL RIGHTS HERO,
JOAN TRUMPAUER MULHOLLAND

LOKI MULHOLLAND

INTERIOR ILLUSTRATIONS BY
CHARLOTTA JANSSEN

SHADOW
MOUNTAIN

To John, Memphis, Annie, Ed, Hank, Luvaghn, Dion,
Reggie, Joyce, Dorie, Stokely, Ruby, Jerry, and Medgar.

—LOKI MULHOLLAND

"Above all else, remember Medgar."

—JOAN TRUMPAUER MULHOLLAND

All photographs and documents courtesy of the Mulholland family, except where noted.
Photograph on page 26 courtesy of Birmingham Civil Rights Institute (BCRI). Used by permission.
Photograph on page 38 courtesy of Fred Blackwell. Used by permission.
Photograph on page 51 © Zack Frank/Shutterstock.com.

Visit us at ShadowMountain.com

Library of Congress Cataloging-in-Publication Data

Names: Mulholland, Loki, author. | Janssen, Charlotta, illustrator.
Title: She stood for freedom : the untold story of a civil rights hero, Joan Trumpauer
    Mulholland / Loki Mulholland ; Illustrated by Charlotta Janssen.
Description: Salt Lake City, Utah : Shadow Mountain, [2016] | ?2016
Identifiers: LCCN 2016000738 | ISBN 9781629721774 (hardbound : alk. paper)
Subjects: LCSH: Mulholland, Joan Trumpauer, 1941- | Civil rights workers—United States—
    Biography. | LCGFT: Biographies.
Classification: LCC E748.M84 M85 2016 | DDC 323.092—dc23 LC record available at http://
    lccn.loc.gov/2016000738

Printed in China   3/2016
RR Donnelley, Shenzhen China

10 9 8 7 6 5 4 3 2 1

INTRODUCTION

I was born in Jackson, Mississippi, in 1945. I grew up in a period of great uncertainty for black people. The lynchings, beatings, and intimidation were all too prevalent. I was eleven years old when Emmett Till was killed. I had learned to not like or trust white people.

In June 1961, the Freedom Rides reached Jackson. I met some white people who not only came down that summer but stayed. That's when I met Joan.

It was a friendship that broke all the rules. Here was this Southern white woman committed to my freedom. How was I to trust her? I knew that any minute she would be gone. I knew that when "her people" got after her, she would sell us down the river. Instead, she made it clear that she was around to stay. I watched her risk her life to live by the principles in which she believed. I felt her take on an unjust system. I felt her embrace the struggle and not give ground to anyone, black or white, who did not have the courage to stand up—a courage I sometimes borrowed.

I would later learn that she had given up her family and friends to live as she thought she should. She knew this and yet she fought.

I came to understand that she never thought of it as my struggle. It belonged to every person of conscience.

As you read her story embrace her as I have. We are her family.

—LUVAGHN BROWN, Freedom Rider

EARLY LIFE FOR JOAN

Ten-year-old Joan was hot and thirsty as she looked out the backseat window. In 1952, cars didn't have air conditioners. The drive from Virginia to Georgia was a long summer trip through the South on U.S. Route 1. Summer was her favorite time of year because she got to visit her Grandma Chandler, her cousins, and her friend Mary. Her grandmother's house, like many in Oconee, was simple. Even though there was running water in the house, it was still best to get drinking water from the well down the dirt road, because sometimes a little fish would make it through the pipes and into your glass.

Joan in Arlington, Virginia, 1942.

LIFE IN THE SOUTH

Joan grew up in Arlington, Virginia, at a time when there was a lot of discrimination and hatred against blacks. They weren't allowed to eat at the same lunch counter, sit in the same part of the bus, or go to the same school as white people. Segregated bathrooms at gas stations and stores were part of everyday life. It was even against the law for whites and blacks to worship together. That was life in the South.

In church, Joan was taught that God loved all of His children (no matter the color of their skin) and that we should treat each other the way we wanted to be treated. In school, Joan's class stood at attention to sing "Dixie," and she memorized the Declaration of Independence, which says "All men are created equal."

Joan, age 10, with her mother, 1951.

THE DIFFERENCE BETWEEN NORTH AND SOUTH

Although the Civil War ended nearly eighty years before Joan was born, there still was a difference in the attitudes toward blacks between the North and the South.

Joan, age 15, with her mother and father, 1956.

Joan's mother was a Southerner, but Joan's father was a Northerner. They had very different attitudes toward black people. Joan's father did not believe black people were inferior to white people. But when Joan's father invited a black person over to dinner, Joan's mother closed herself in the kitchen and would not come out.

This was the difference between being taught that blacks were equals and being taught that blacks were inferior. Joan would see this attitude many times in her life.

SEGREGATION

In the South, people were taught that segregation was the will of God. Red birds and blue birds didn't mix. Each stuck to their own kind. People should do the same. Some people believed that blacks were not fully human, that they did not have a soul that could be "saved" by God.

Race Mixing is a dumb, stupid, unnatural action. Even the animals, birds, and fish know better than to mix.

Race mixing is an outrageous action and WILL result in mongrelization, degradation and destruction of white Christian America and Civilization.

Race mixing is a Subversive device in the Communistic plot to destroy White America and Christianity.

If you preach, teach, or advocate race mixing, you are promoting the communist line and the religion of the Devil.

If you are a patriotic, Christian White American you will heed this message and have copies printed and distributed to ministers and professors.

Hate mail Joan received while she was a student at Tougaloo College, 1961.

THE RULES

The long summer days in Georgia offered Joan and Mary great opportunities for adventure but the rules were clear: they were not allowed to go beyond the Coca-Cola bottling plant, and the black area was absolutely forbidden.

"Let's go," said Mary.

"I don't want to," replied Joan. "We can't go there. Grandma said so."

"Come on," urged Mary. "I dare you."

Joan knew she was breaking the rules, but Mary had dared her. So hand in hand, they went down the dirt road with the railroad track running down the middle and turned off to where the blacks lived.

THE SCHOOLHOUSE

Joan's grandmother was poor, but not as poor as the blacks in Oconee.

"I think the people here are afraid of us," Joan whispered to Mary. She thought it was strange that no one wanted to be seen anywhere near them and hid themselves behind their houses and doors.

When Joan and Mary reached the black schoolhouse, Joan stopped and stared. It was not like the brand-new brick school for the white children. This was a one-room unpainted shack on stone piles with a potbellied stove in the middle for warmth, and an outhouse and hand-pump in the dirt school yard.

Joan's soul was rattled. This was not fair. She knew, despite what her family and society believed, that separating people and treating them differently because of the color of their skin was wrong. She decided she was going to do something about it when she had the chance.

SEGREGATION IN SCHOOL

In 1954, the United States Supreme Court ruled in a case known as Brown v. the Board of Education that segregated schools were unconstitutional. Joan's home state of Virginia was one of many Southern states that resisted the ruling. Virginia passed a state law that said if a single school in a school district were integrated (meaning blacks and whites attended the same school), the entire school district could be closed down by the governor.

A girl in Joan's eleventh grade Spanish class had missed a year of school because her school had been shut down. Other white families had to move into other school districts so their children could finish their education. That caused Joan and her friends to consider what could happen and what was most important. If schools closed, they wouldn't get their high school diplomas, move on to college, and get good jobs. She, along with many of her classmates, didn't care if the schools integrated—they just wanted to have a school open so they could graduate.

YOUTH DINNER AT CHURCH

Around the same time (about 1958), Joan's youth pastor told them that black students would be joining their Sunday night spaghetti dinner. They had to keep it a secret. If anyone found out, they could all be arrested or the church attacked.

Joan had been around black people her entire life. There were those who helped clean the house and the yard, and she had a black nanny when she was a baby, but this was different.

The church curtains were drawn as the white and black teenagers met in the basement. The students didn't know what to say when they first sat down at the table together. As they began to eat, their chatter filled the air. Joan learned that black students and white students really weren't all that different.

Joan kept her involvement in that activity a secret for more than fifty years.

FROM HIGH SCHOOL TO COLLEGE

Joan graduated from Annandale High in 1959. She wanted to go to a small church college. But her mother insisted on Duke University because it was a well-known and segregated school. She didn't want her daughter to have "colored" classmates or a roommate who was black.

Senior Picture 1959

Joan began attending Duke in the fall. The next spring, black students from North Carolina College invited white Duke students to join their demonstrations against segregation in Durham, North Carolina. A demonstration is a chance for people to get together in public and show they feel strongly about a cause. Joan saw it as a way to try to change people's opinions about segregation, but she knew that if she did, her family in Georgia might never speak to her again. She would never be able to go back to the life she knew.

Could she do what was right even if it wasn't easy?

Joan joined the Civil Rights Movement in 1960. Thousands of other people from across the South and the nation were standing up for equal rights for everyone.

DUKE UNIVERSITY —
N.C. COLLEGE

INTERRACIAL COMMITTEE MEETING

The Ark — East Campus
8:00 pm Sunday April 24

AGENDA:

1. Report on developments in Durham

2. Report on Raleigh Meeting

3. Report on Picnic Plans

Report on Picketing in Durham

BRING OTHERS TO THIS MEETING WHO ARE INTERESTED IN WORKING WITH US

This flyer inspired Joan to join the Civil Rights Movement, 1960.

Joan with fellow demonstrators in Durham, North Carolina.

IN JOAN'S WORDS

"People ask, 'Why you?' The question I ask is 'Why not me?'

"I joined the Civil Rights Movement because it seemed the right thing to do. I'd already reached the point where I knew that segregation was wrong. As a Southerner, I felt I should do my part to make things better. This was my chance to change things. To make the South better.

"I don't think you're ever really totally aware of the consequences of your actions. We knew we could be arrested; we knew we probably would be arrested. But where it would go from there—I didn't know.

"But I couldn't make a difference if I did nothing, and they were asking us to step forward, so I did."

BACKLASH FROM DUKE UNIVERSITY

When Joan began to participate in sit-ins and other demonstrations, the administration at Duke University was concerned and confused. Why would a Southern white woman do this kind of thing? They branded her a "radical" and insisted she call her parents to tell them what she was doing. Joan didn't let the backlash from her school stop her from doing what she felt was right.

Joan as a college student, 1960.

1960: A SUMMER OF DEMONSTRATIONS

Under pressure from the school, Joan eventually left Duke University and returned to Virginia. She joined Howard University students in sit-ins in her home town of Arlington. A sit-in is a special kind of demonstration where people sit on seats at a segregated lunch counter until they are served or arrested.

HOW A SIT-IN WORKED

White students generally entered the store first and made a small purchase—school supplies or a candy bar. It was important to keep the cash register receipt in order to be identified as a welcomed customer. Then the students would sit down at the lunch counter and order something to eat.

When the food would arrive, black students would join the white students at the counter. If the seats were limited, the white student would often give up the seat to the black student.

If the black student was refused service, the white student would offer the food off his or her plate.

Then, in Joan's words, "You sit. You try not to focus on the unpleasantness going on around you. You help keep each other's nerves together. You wait to see what will happen. The police don't want to intervene without a reason. The management doesn't want to be in the position of ordering an arrest."

If someone was knocked off or pulled off the stool, they would simply try to regain the seat.

If there was a violent reaction to the sit-in, the manager would call the police. The manager would declare the counter "Closed" and remove all the unoccupied seats. The demonstrating students would often be arrested and taken to jail.

If the police were not called, everyone remained in the store until it closed.

Receipt from milk that Joan purchased to establish herself as a customer, 1960.

Joan's handwritten notes of a sit-in demonstration, 1960.

That summer Joan and her friends demonstrated all over the Washington, DC, area, including at Glen Echo Park, the local segregated amusement park in Maryland.

Joan and her friends worked with the community who wanted the swimming pools to be open to everyone. Sometimes, Joan would purchase tickets for the rides at the amusement park and hand them out to her black friends. The most popular ride was the merry-go-round, because, as the poet Langston Hughes wrote, "There ain't no back / to a merry-go-round."

When her friends were arrested for being on the ride, Joan and her friends picketed the park. But nothing would fully prepare Joan for what would take place in 1961.

ATTENTION
AMERICANS:

THE OWNERS OF GLEN ECHO AMUSEMENT PARK DISCRIMINATE AGAINST YOUR FELLOW CITIZENS. ALL NEGROES ARE BARRED FROM THIS PARK. WE BELIEVE THIS IS NOT THE WILL OF THE MAJORITY OF ITS PATRONS.

WILL YOU SPEAK OUT FOR EQUALITY? YOU CAN ADVANCE DEMOCRACY BY SPEAKING OUT AND LETTING THE MANAGERS KNOW YOU WISH THEM TO CHANGE THEIR POLICY. DEMOCRACY IS EVERYBODY'S BUSINESS.

UNTIL THE STAIN OF RACIAL DISCRIMINATION IS REMOVED -- THIS PARK IS A SHAME TO OUR NATION'S CAPITAL.

DIRECT YOUR PROTEST TO:

MR. SAMUEL BAKER AND MR. ABRAM BAKER
GLEN ECHO AMUSEMENT PARK
GLEN ECHO, MARYLAND

HOW A JAIL-IN WORKED

A jail-in was another way to draw attention to the cause of the Civil Rights Movement. Many people involved in demonstrations were arrested and sent to jail. The idea behind a jail-in was that the people who were arrested would not appeal their sentence. They would stay in jail. The more people who were arrested, the more people would fill up the jail, eventually overloading the system. They hoped people would see what the protestors were sacrificing and be more willing to talk about the issues.

HINDS COUNTY JAIL
JACKSON, MISSISSIPPI

You, *Joan Harris Trumpower*, have been committed to the Hinds County Jail by order of Judge *James Spencer*

for the crime of *Breach of the Peace*

Your sentence has been set at $ *200.00* and or *4 Months 3 Months suspended*

You will be released from this Jail: Month *Oct* Day *12th* Year 19 *61*

J. R. GILFOY
Sheriff of Hinds County

By *Jim Kelly*
Deputy Sheriff

*Joan received this conviction and sentencing document
for her involvement in the Freedom Rides, 1961.*

Telegram Joan received while in jail in South Carolina, 1961.

IN JOAN'S WORDS

"The movement became family. Once you stepped outside the bounds of acceptability, there was no stepping back. You could only go forward. Black kids sometimes couldn't go back, either, not because their parents disowned them, but because it wasn't safe. They were asked not to come back. They knew they or their parents could be killed, or their homes burned down. So for a lot of us, there was no turning back, and we became family."

FREEDOM RIDES

It was a warm day in May 1961 when two interstate buses rolled out of Washington, DC. The regular passengers were joined by a group of black and white passengers headed to New Orleans. They were the Freedom Riders. They wanted to draw attention to unjust segregation in the South and test the Supreme Court's ruling that there could not be segregation in interstate travel.

Joan joked with her friend, Hank Thomas, that he was getting an all-expense paid vacation without really protesting.

But when photos appeared in the newspaper, Joan was speechless. There was Hank standing in front of his burning bus in Anniston, Alabama, on Mother's Day. The Freedom Riders had gotten attention—but not the kind they were hoping for. The Freedom Rides seemed all but over.

ATTACKING THE BUS

The picture of the burning bus has become an iconic image of the Freedom Rides. Joan recalls what happened:

"We knew what happened from the newspapers. When the bus was stopped at the station in Anniston, folks who were not favorable toward the Freedom Riders slashed the tires. Then, as the bus drove out of town, the tires went flat. The bus was boxed in by cars in the front and cars in the back; the bus didn't have anywhere to go.

"Once the tires went flat, the bus driver walked away, but the doors were kept closed by the mob. A fire bomb exploded, and there was a big fire. People stumbled off the bus, but this bus

CAN A NEGRO AMERICAN
TAKE A FREEDOM RIDE...?

Negro and white Americans, members of CORE, are travelling by Greyhound and by Trailways bus between Washington, D.C. and New Orleans. They call their trip the "Freedom Ride." They have been beaten, jim-crowed, and thrown into jail because they tried to practice what the Federal government and the bus companies preach. The law and company policy state that all passengers are entitled to equal accommodations and equal treatment. For attempting to obtain such accomodations and treatment, "Freedom Riders" have felt chains in the face and the terror of mob violence.

WE ACCUSE the Greyhound and Trailways Bus Companies of discriminating against colored citizens and their white companions.

WE ACCUSE these companies of selling tickets in bad faith.

WE ACCUSE these companies of violation of Federal laws governing transportation in interstate commerce.

Can you sit content while this unfair treatment of your fellow citizens goes on?

Do you want to do something against discrimination based on race, creed, color, or national origin?

If you do, we urge you to:

* Protest to Greyhound and Trailways Bus Companies.

* Protest to the Attorney General, insisting that the power of the Department of Justice be used to enforce the law as interpreted by the Supreme Court.

* Support the Washington CONGRESS OF RACIAL EQUALITY, an organization dedicated to social change through peaceful, non-violent means. We invite you to the next meeting of CORE. Regular meetings are held every other Tuesday in the ALLIANCE ROOM of ALL SOULS CHURCH, 16th and Harvard Streets, N.W. Next meeting: May 23, 1961

8 P.M.

NO AMERICAN CAN CALL HIMSELF FREE WHILE
ANY AMERICAN IS DEPRIVED OF FREEDOM

25

didn't have just Freedom Riders. It had other passengers, too. Fortunately nobody was killed."

It wasn't until decades later that Joan learned more of the story.

The burning bus had been forced to stop near a small grocery store owned by a white family. The owners' twelve-year-old daughter, Janie Miller, saw people stumbling out of the bus, gasping and coughing. Janie took water to the people who were choking. She went from one to the next, giving them water and comforting them. Because she chose to help the Freedom Riders, the "Angel of Anniston" was forced to leave her family and the town.

Hank Thomas, standing by a bus he was on when it was bombed during the Freedom Rides, May 14, 1961.

POLICE DEPT.
JACKSON, MISS
20975
6-8-61

ARRESTED

Students from across the South came to Alabama to keep the Freedom Rides going. One of the nonviolent principles behind the Freedom Rides was that if one person fell, another would stand to take their place.

Joan and some of her friends flew to New Orleans, took a train to Jackson, Mississippi, and went into the train station together. They were arrested and sent to Hinds County Jail. The jail was hot and full of other students from all over the country. Joan kept a diary hidden in the hem of her skirt.

Life in the county jail became almost routine when rumors started spreading that they would soon be heading to the most notorious prison in America: Parchman.

EXCERPT FROM JOAN'S DIARY

"Friday, June 9th. They were bringing in the food as I was waking up. Jane and Betty were asleep, but we woke them about halfway through breakfast. Grits and gravy, four stewed prunes, 3 hot biscuits. We roll the beds up and put them around the spare wall spaces. They give us a broom and a mop with disinfectant. . . . We've got a clothesline strung up. Camera straps and ripped up handkerchiefs. They collect mail in the morning. Also today some of us are making phone calls and getting our clothes."

ROSS BARNETT, GOVERNOR
TOM ROSS
CHAIRMAN, BOARD OF COMMISSIONERS

WALKER SCRUGGS
COMMISSIONER

WILLIAM L. HUDSON
COMMISSIONER

Mississippi State Penitentiary

FRED JONES
SUPERINTENDENT

MINGA LAWRENCE
ASSISTANT SUPERINTENDENT

J. D. SISTRUNK
AGRONOMIST

T. D. MIDDLETON
FARM MANAGER

OLEN C. POUND
ANIMAL HUSBANDMAN

F. H. LINSKEY
SECRETARY

R. L. PATTERSON, JR.
EDUCATIONAL DIRECTOR

J. P. HENRY
CLASSIFICATION OFFICER

R. W. McGUFFEE
HORTICULTURIST

PARCHMAN, MISSISSIPPI

12th
July
1961

Mrs. Merle Nelson
5150 Wilson Blvd.
Arlington 5, Virginia

Dear Mrs. Nelson:

I have your letter in regard to your daughter Joan Trumpower.

If there is any medicine that you want her to have, if you will send it we will see that she gets it.

Your daughter is receiving plenty of food, has been provided with a tooth brush, tooth paste and whatever else she actually needs.

I notice that you state that as a mother of a minor that you want to be notified in case of any emergency. What I cannot understand is why as a mother you permitted a minor white girl to gang up with a bunch of negro bucks and white hoodlums to ramble over this country with the express purpose of violating the laws of certain states and attempting to incite acts of violence.

If you are concerned enough, you could post bond for your daughter and have her released. Such action will have to be taken up with the Sheriff of Hinds County, Jackson, Mississippi.

Very truly,

Fred Jones, Superintendent

FJ:mk

Letter Joan's mother received from the superintendent
of Parchman Penitentiary, 1961.

PARCHMAN PRISON

The old state prison farm was deep in the Mississippi Delta, far from the press and from safety. Rumors said that people never returned from Parchman, and the few that did were never quite the same. All Joan and her companions could do was pray as the truck they were transported in drove along the lonely two-lane highway.

At Parchman, the prisoners were housed on Death Row, men and women in separate cell blocks. The cells were segregated by race. There could be up to four people in the tiny cells, but usually there were only two. Joan was issued a coarse denim black-and-white striped skirt and T-shirt. She was taken to cell number fourteen, where she would spend the next two months, all because she was trying to do what was right.

Fifty years later, she would learn that her cell had been around the corner from the death chamber.

Joan, visiting her cell at Parchman Penitentiary on the 50th anniversary of the Freedom Rides, 2011.

FROM: Rabbi Perry E. Nussbaum, Beth Israel Congregation, P. O. Box 4766
Fondren Station, Jackson 6, Mississippi

~~July 28, 1961~~ August 4, 1961

Dear Friend(s):

When I visited Parchman Penitentiary yesterday JOAN TRUMPOWER
asked me to write you that he (or she) is in good health, good spirits and sends
you deep affection. In particular, you are asked not to worry.

I realize that the above statement in a form letter is subject to question,
but I hope that the knowledge that your dear one has been seen by a Rabbi – who
expects to make weekly visits – will compensate for the generalities.

For what it is worth, I have been a Chaplain in the military and in all
kinds of civilian institutions for more than a quarter of a century. I do not
assume to be an authority on penal conditions at our State institution, but I
do believe your dear one is in good shape, physically and spiritually. This
impression is the result of meeting with them (in which quite a few non-Jews

RABBI NUSSBAUM

Rabbi Nussbaum visited the prison faithfully every week. Because of his service to those involved in the Civil Rights Movement, he was a marked man. His synagogue had been attacked and threats had been made against him. But he still drove to the prison every week. Same route, same time.

The wardens would call out "Who wants to hear the rabbi? Who wants to pray with the rabbi?" Joan was a Presbyterian, but she would still call out her cell number. "A man of God is a man of God," she believed. She liked Rabbi Nussbaum's visits not only because it gave her a chance to be out of her cell, but also because after the rabbi had prayed for a while in Hebrew, and the guards were no longer paying attention, he would be able to tell the prisoners some of the world news. The rabbi was also able to deliver some personal messages from family members to the prisoners.

In Joan's words, "It was good to be with a man of God."

TOUGALOO COLLEGE

After she was released from Parchman, Joan stayed in Mississippi and attended Tougaloo College, a historically black school.

Not everyone was happy that Joan was there. Some of the students didn't trust her motives. Joan received letters in the mail from both people who supported her and people who said she was a traitor. The state of Mississippi even tried to close Tougaloo College because of Joan, but because the school's charter predated the "Jim Crow laws"—state and local laws enforcing racial segregation—they couldn't.

Joan went to classes and studied hard. In 1962, she was invited by her friend, Joyce Ladner, to join the all-black sorority (a student organization for women) Delta Sigma Theta. She even got to meet Dr. Martin Luther King Jr.

Dr. Martin Luther King Jr.'s autograph, 1962.

Joan with Dr. Martin Luther King Jr. at Tougaloo College in Mississippi, 1962.

BEING A WHITE WOMAN AT A BLACK COLLEGE

It was unusual for a white woman to attend a black college, but Joan didn't feel out of place. She had spent so much time around blacks that she realized she had a lot in common with them. She and her friends had been through the sit-ins together. They enjoyed the same food. They had the same kind of religious upbringing.

Joan said, "The white students who came from the North had a lot to get used to. I was at home."

And the longer she was at college, and the more people saw her studying in the library and eating in the cafeteria, or heard her complaining about the same things that all college students complained about, she felt more and more accepted on campus.

"By the time I came back my second year," Joan recalled. "I was pretty much just another student. Some folks liked me, some folks didn't, but that's true of anybody."

A GHOST SIGHTING: IN JOAN'S WORDS

"The students knew the Freedom Riders were around, and having white people come to campus was not so unusual; probably half of the professors were white and their families were on campus. But being a white girl in an all-black dormitory was new and different.

"I ended up in one of the larger dormitory rooms. There were two sets of bunk beds so we were a bit crowded that first night. Students were still arriving and not everyone was aware

I was there. I was tiptoeing down the dimly-lit hallway to the bathroom, wearing a pale, flowing nightgown just as another student was tiptoeing down the hallway from the other direction. She saw me and screamed. She thought she was seeing a ghost!

"We eventually made it back to our dorm rooms and had a good laugh about it. The next morning, the whole dorm knew there was a white girl on campus."

Gamma Psi Chapter
Delta Sigma Theta Sorority
Tougaloo College
Tougaloo, Miss.

DELTA SIGMA THETA SORORITY, INC.

FORM C

Date *November 29, 1962*

(State name and address of Addressee)

My dear (Miss or Mrs.) *Joan Trumpauer*
Tougaloo College

It is with a great deal of pleasure, that Delta Sigma Theta Sorority extends to you an invitation to membership through

Gamma Psi Chapter;

If you are interested, we shall be glad to give you further details as to candidacy for membership.

May we hear from you by *3:00 P.M.* today (*written statement*)

Yours truly,

Bobbie Gray
Chapter President

Lynette Anderson
Chapter Secretary

Kindly reply (name) *Joyce A. Ladner*, Membership Committee Chairman
Address *Galloway Hall*
Tougaloo College

Joan's invitation to become a member of Delta Sigma Theta Sorority, Inc., 1962.

RUBBING ELBOWS WITH THE STARS

Tougaloo was a magnet for anybody who wanted to show support for the movement. In some circles it became a status symbol to have spoken or performed at Tougaloo. There was no other place in Mississippi where audiences could be integrated.

During the years Joan attended Tougaloo, the singer-songwriter Bob Dylan, the undersecretary of the United Nations Ralph Bunche, and the author James Baldwin were among those who came to the campus to show their support. Joan Baez even gave a concert on campus.

During the Civil Rights Movement, Joan met a number of famous people, including Jessie Owens, Jackie Robinson, Fannie Lou Hamer, John Lewis, Robert F. Kennedy, James Meredith, Ralph Abernathy, and Andrew Young.

JOAN BAEZ

TOUGALOO COLLEGE
TOUGALOO, MISSISSIPPI

April 5, 1964   7:00 p.m.

Admission

STUDENT: At the Door $1.50
            Advance $1.00

NON-STUDENT: At the Door $2.00
                Advance $1.50

A DANGEROUS PLACE TO WALK

One day, Joan and a black civil rights worker were walking from downtown Jackson back toward the black community. To be safe, they deliberately walked on opposite sides of the street. Once they reached the black community, it was less dangerous for a white woman and a black man to walk together.

Suddenly, a car filled with white people drove through the black community. They spotted Joan and her friend, stopped the car, and started chasing them with a tire iron. The pair split up, Joan going into a Salvation Army store where she hid under a table. Her friend darted across the street, up the steps of a nearby house, and then out the back door, cutting through backyards until he reached the civil rights office. The store owners sheltered Joan until it was safe.

After the incident, Joan and the others talked about what had happened, questioning if it could have been avoided had they started walking together at another place in the black community. They concluded that it had happened because a car full of white people was in the black community. Joan knew that to stop events like that from happening again, the Civil Rights Movement must move forward.

SIT-IN AT WOOLWORTH'S

Woolworth's was a chain of inexpensive "five-and-dime" stores with lunch counters. Students in the South had been protesting segregation laws by holding sit-in demonstrations at such stores since 1960. Some had been peaceful. Others had not. No one thought the May 28, 1963, sit-in at the Woolworth's lunch counter in Jackson, Mississippi, was going to be a big deal.

John Salter, Joan, and Anne Moody at the Woolworth's lunch counter, 1963.

John Salter, a professor at Tougaloo College, and Medgar Evers, the field secretary for the National Association for the Advancement of Colored People (NAACP), planned it. Students Pearlena Lewis, Anne Moody, and Memphis Norman were ready to be the first group of black customers to sit at the lunch counter. But things didn't go as planned.

The three students sat down, but were pulled off their stools. Memphis was pulled to the floor and severely beaten before being arrested. Joan took his place, but then she and her friend Anne were pulled off their stools and pushed toward to the store entrance. They broke free and returned to the counter. Other demonstrators had also come to the counter.

An angry crowd of white high school students formed. They started to dump sugar and mustard on Joan and her friends.

"You no-good traitor!" an angry white man shouted at Joan. "You went against your own race."

Joan later said, "I wasn't really afraid. I was beyond fear. I think I was just driven by determination to carry this through."

The mob of more than two hundred people screamed at Joan, Anne, and Professor Salter as they sat at the counter. Joan didn't think any of them were going to make it out alive, but after three hours, the police finally escorted them safely out of the store.

THE MARCH ON WASHINGTON

After school ended for the summer, Joan went to Washington, DC, and started working on another large demonstration that was being organized. She hoped the March on Washington would be a success. She hoped that it would help bring civil rights to everyone.

On the morning of August 28, 1963, nearly 250,000 Americans—including Joan—listened as Martin Luther King Jr.

Cards, badges, and stickers from the Civil Rights Movement.

spoke on the steps of the Lincoln Memorial. It would become known everywhere as the "I Have a Dream" speech.

During part of his speech, he said, "I have a dream that my four little children will one day live in a nation where they will not be judged by the color of their skin but by the content of their character."

It was a dream that Joan and many others believed in. Joan promised herself that she would continue work to achieve that dream, no matter how long it took.

IN JOAN'S WORDS

"A lot of people were against the Civil Rights Movement, and even up to the morning of the march, we were not at all certain it was going to happen. The newspaper warned of riots; store owners boarded up their storefronts. Some people feared that the federal government might bring troops to prevent the March from happening by stopping the buses before they got to the city. But then we went down by the Lincoln Memorial early in the morning and saw the buses beginning to appear. Everything was peaceful and beautiful. That was a good moment.

"Many people don't know that in Dr. King's prepared speech he did not have his 'I Have a Dream' speech that we're all fa-miliar with now. That was added, sort of as an inspiration, at the end. It's interesting to me now that his speech has become so iconic, but at the time the Washington Post's *lead story about the March featured A. Philip Randolf as the number one speaker."*

A BOMB AND A FUNERAL

Less than three weeks later, however, on September 15, men belonging to the Ku Klux Klan—a violent group who believed that white people were better than black people and that the two races should not mix—planted a bomb at the 16th Street Baptist Church in Birmingham, Alabama. When it exploded, it killed four little black girls who were preparing for a special Youth Sunday program. The church lesson that day was "The Love That Forgives."

Joan and some of her friends traveled from Tougaloo to Birmingham for the funeral. They picked up some pieces of the shattered stained glass from the church windows as well as some casings from police bullets.

Dr. King spoke at the funeral. So many people came that Joan and her friends had to listen to loudspeakers outside on the street. The National Guard thought there would be a violent demonstration. They stood on the rooftops with guns pointed at the funeral goers, but the people were only thinking about those little girls.

Fragments of stained glass that Joan collected after the bombing, 1963.

Joan would later say that it was the saddest day of the Civil Rights Movement when they buried those little girls.

THE HONEST TRUTH IN LOUISIANA

It was dangerous to ride in a car when the occupants were both black and white. Joan often rode with a black scarf on her head to hide her hair, or she would sometimes have to ride on the floor of the car, covered by a blanket or a coat and other people's feet.

There was one car trip where Joan and her friends had to drive through the rough parts of Louisiana. They decided that if they were stopped, they would tell the police that Joan's father was white. This would explain why her skin was much lighter than the others'.

As luck would have it, they did get stopped. The policemen separated Joan from the others, but the group stuck to the story: Joan's father was white. One of the policemen asked about her mother, and Joan replied, "Well, she's part Indian, and my father's white." This was actually the honest truth. Joan's mother's family heritage had Native American blood.

Because Joan had said she wasn't completely white, the police finally let them go. Joan and her friends weren't arrested or hurt. They were able to continue their journey to Baton Rouge, where Joan was jailed for contempt of court for sitting in the "colored" section of the courtroom.

THE DANGERS OF DEMONSTRATING

Joan had had brushes with death before. She was chased by angry white men in Jackson. Shots were fired in Arlington and Durham. Police dogs lunged at her in the garage of the Jackson jail. When a group of angry men stopped the car she was riding in outside of Canton, Mississippi, one evening in May 1964, she thought her time had come.

The men began beating on the car, trying to get Joan and the others. The mob had already picked out a place to kill them. She, like several others, was on the Ku Klux Klan's "Most Wanted" list. The Klan believed that killing Joan and the other people in the Civil Rights Movement would stop blacks from seeking the right to vote. Voting meant things would change, and they didn't want things to change.

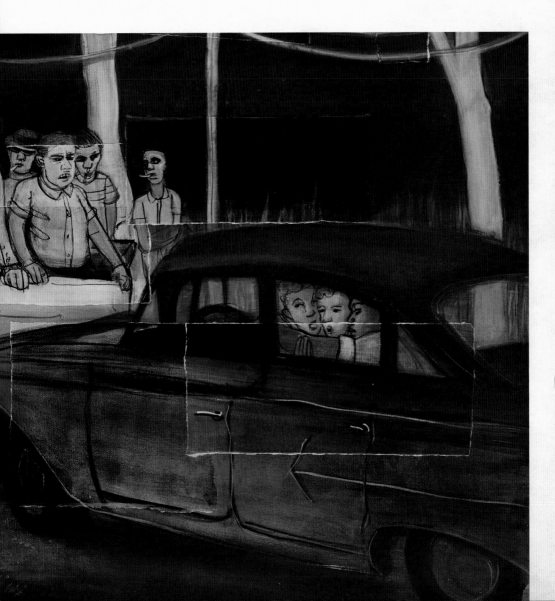

THE LOSS OF FRIENDS

When students came from the North to join the Civil Rights Movement, they often went to orientation at Tougaloo College. Joan was one of the people who gave them the "What you need to know as white Civil Rights workers in Mississippi" orientation. She felt a closeness to them, especially since she knew the risks of standing for freedom. Her friend Bob Moses once asked her, "Can we ask these students to do this if we know that some of them might die?"

It was a hard question to answer, especially after three of the workers went missing. Their disappearance became a very big case with the Federal Bureau of Investigation (FBI). When the news came that the three workers had died, she was left with a feeling that she had to work doubly hard because her friends were no longer there to do it.

In later years, Joan was asked if she felt guilt for being alive when others died. "Guilt is not the word," she said. "There's nothing I could have said or done that would have made any difference in the way things turned out. I'm clear on that. Those of us who are left to keep up the good fight have to do a little extra for them. To promote the brotherhood of man and peace."

Three students who were killed for trying to help others, 1964.

WHY ARE YOU DOING THIS?

Joan was asked many times why she was putting her life in danger for the Civil Rights movement. Why had she left her family and friends and her old way of life, to fight for the cause?

Joan's response, at least to herself, was a poem she wrote called "Dialogue."

This poem, Joan said, is "still my response. It still explains my attitude toward what I've done on the Civil Rights issue, primarily motivated by being a Southerner and a Christian, and incidentally, an American."

```
                        Dialogue

        Where have you been?

        To jail.

        What did you do?

        Nothing.
        Nothing but act like an American.

        Why did you do that?
        I thought you were a Southerner.

        I am.

        Yes.
        Then why?

        That's why.
        Because I'm a Southerner.

        Nothing more??

        I'm a Christian.

        That's what they all say.
        But for a different reason.

        I read the Declaration of Independence.

        You are strange.

        Yes.

        Very strange.

        But not alone.
```

"NEVER QUIT"

Joan survived and continued to support the Civil Rights Movement, but not all of her friends were so lucky. Some of them were killed. Joan knew that the work she and her friends did helped give the activists in the Civil Rights Movement the strength to press forward. They knew that good always triumphed over evil. They would succeed, as long as they never quit.

Joan graduated from Tougaloo College in 1964 and a few years later started a family. She continued to participate in events like the Selma to Montgomery March in 1965 and the Meredith March in 1966. The day President Lyndon B. Johnson said, "And we *shall* overcome," was a powerful moment for Joan. Everyone would now have the opportunity to vote.

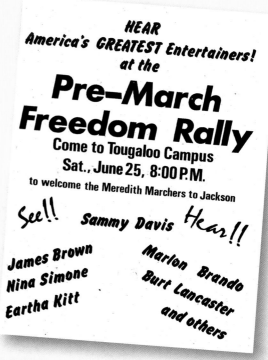

HEAR
America's GREATEST Entertainers!
at the
Pre–March Freedom Rally
Come to Tougaloo Campus
Sat., June 25, 8:00 P.M.
to welcome the Meredith Marchers to Jackson

See!! Sammy Davis Hear!!

James Brown
Nina Simone
Eartha Kitt

Marlon Brando
Burt Lancaster
and others

WORKING AT THE SMITHSONIAN

For a time, Joan worked as a typist at the Smithsonian Institution. The American History Museum was just opening, but the museum had virtually nothing on black history. Joan was asked to use her contacts to find some appropriate items that would represent African-American culture. She reached out to her friends and gathered some items related to the Civil Rights Movement: a deck of cards made out of envelopes, some picket signs from North Carolina, a burned cross. Joan even donated her personal bib skirt that she had worn in Mississippi.

Smithsonian Institution.

LASTING FRIENDSHIPS

Joan made many friends during the years she fought for Civil Rights. One such friend was a black student from Howard University named Stokely Carmichael. He and Joan went on the same Freedom Ride, taking a train from New Orleans to Jackson. In later years, he became a famous leader in the Black Power movement, which some believed promoted a more violent form of demonstrating.

Joan went to hear him speak at the Smithsonian and approached him after the speech. He was surrounded by bodyguards, and he stood well over six feet tall. However, when he saw Joan with her children, he called them over. In front of everyone, he knelt on the floor so he could talk to Joan's children face to face and shake their hands.

He went out of his way to acknowledge her and made it clear that his friends were her friends. "We were friends right to the end," Joan said.

"AN ORDINARY HERO"

Joan became a teacher's assistant in Arlington, Virginia, and made sure her kids learned the lesson she knew was most important: "You can never go wrong by doing what is right. It might not be easy, but it is always right."

Many people say Joan is a hero, but she'll tell you she is not. She says, "I'm as ordinary as they come. I saw something was wrong and decided to do something about it. It takes all of us to make a difference. We just have to make the choice."

What can you do? You can do the same thing Joan did when she was a little girl in Georgia. She decided to do what was right.

"You don't need to be a Dr. King or a Rosa Parks," Joan says. "Everyone can make a difference, right where they are. Sometimes you don't know when you're going to be making a difference, or how big of a difference, or what direction it will go. When something is the right thing to do, DO IT! It's that simple.

"It doesn't matter how old or young you are. Find a problem, get some friends together, and go fix it. We can all make life better. Be true to yourself. Do what's right. Make the world a better place.

"Remember, you don't have to change the world . . . just change *your* world."

CIVIL RIGHTS TIMELINE

April 15, 1947—Jackie Robinson breaks the "color barrier" and becomes the first black Major League Baseball player.

July 26, 1948—President Truman orders integration of the armed forces.

May 17, 1954—Brown v. Board of Education. Supreme Court rules schools must be integrated. Separate is not equal.

August 28, 1955—Emmett Till, a fourteen-year-old boy, is tortured and killed after being accused of whistling at a white woman.

December 1, 1955—Rosa Parks is arrested for refusing to move to the back of a city bus. Reverend Martin Luther King Jr. leads the Montgomery Bus Boycott.

September 25, 1957—Nine students integrate Central High School in Little Rock, Arkansas.

February 1, 1960—Student lunch counter sit-ins are held throughout the South, beginning in Greensboro, North Carolina.

April 15-17, 1960—Students form the Student Nonviolent Coordinating Committee (SNCC).

November 14, 1960—Ruby Bridges becomes the first black student to attend an all-white elementary school in Louisiana.

May 4, 1961—People participating in the Freedom Rides board buses, trains, and planes to obtain equal treatment in interstate travel (as required by the Supreme Court). Hundreds go to jail.

October 1, 1962—James Meredith becomes the first black student to enroll at the University of Mississippi.

May 2-5, 1963—The Children's Crusade—a march made by hundreds of school students—is attacked by police dogs and fire hoses in Birmingham, Alabama.

May 28, 1963—Sit-in held at a Woolworth's lunch counter in Jackson, Mississippi, is attacked.

June 12, 1963—Civil rights leader Medgar Evers is assassinated in Jackson, Mississippi.

August 27, 1963—Dr. Martin Luther King Jr. leads the March on Washington.

September 15, 1963—Four girls are killed in the bombing of the 16th Street Baptist Church in Birmingham, Alabama.

November 22, 1963—President John F. Kennedy is assassinated in Dallas, Texas.

January 23, 1964—The 24th Amendment abolishes poll taxes.

Summer 1964—Known as "Freedom Summer" in Mississippi. Hundreds of students work for civil rights. Three are killed.

July 2, 1964—Civil Rights Act of 1964 becomes law, outlawing discrimination based on race, color, or religion.

August 24-27, 1964—Fannie Lou Hamer and other members of the Mississippi Freedom Democratic Party demand to be seated at the Democratic National Convention in Atlantic City, New Jersey.

February 21, 1965—Civil Rights leader Malcolm X is assassinated in Harlem, New York.

March 7, 1965—Demonstrators attempt to cross the Edmund Pettus Bridge in Selma, Alabama, but are attacked and beaten by police.

August 6, 1965—President Lyndon B. Johnson signs the Voting Rights Act of 1965 into law.

June 6, 1966—James Meredith begins the March Against Fear from Memphis, Tennessee, to Jackson, Mississippi. He is shot on the second day of the march. Thousands rally to finish the march for him.

April 4, 1968—Civil Rights leader Martin Luther King Jr. is assassinated in Memphis, Tennessee.